*Plan your work
and work your plan*

This planner belongs to:

_____

Week _____ *Year* _____

MONDAY	TUESDAY	WEDNESDAY

Quote of the Week: *The best way to predict your future is to create it.*

THURSDAY	FRIDAY	WEEKEND

Week _____ *Year* _____

MONDAY	TUESDAY	WEDNESDAY

Quote of the Week: *Practice like you've never won. Perform like you've never lost.*

THURSDAY	FRIDAY	WEEKEND

Week _____ *Year* _____

MONDAY	TUESDAY	WEDNESDAY

Quote of the Week: *You get in life what you have the courage to ask for.*

THURSDAY	FRIDAY	WEEKEND

Week _____ *Year* _____

MONDAY	TUESDAY	WEDNESDAY

Quote of the Week: *Doubt kills more dreams than failure ever will.*

THURSDAY	FRIDAY	WEEKEND

Week _____ *Year* _____

MONDAY	TUESDAY	WEDNESDAY

Quote of the Week: *The best project you'll ever work on is yourself.*

THURSDAY	FRIDAY	WEEKEND

Week _____ *Year* _____

MONDAY	TUESDAY	WEDNESDAY

Quote of the Week: *Keep your eyes on the stars and your feet on the ground.*

THURSDAY	FRIDAY	WEEKEND

Week _____ *Year* _____

MONDAY	TUESDAY	WEDNESDAY

Quote of the Week: *Your speed doesn't matter. Forward is forward.*

THURSDAY	FRIDAY	WEEKEND

Week _____ *Year* _____

MONDAY	TUESDAY	WEDNESDAY

Quote of the Week: *The grass is always greener where you water it.*

THURSDAY	FRIDAY	WEEKEND

Week _____ *Year* _____

MONDAY	TUESDAY	WEDNESDAY

Quote of the Week: *Believe in yourself like your life depends on it. It does.*

THURSDAY	FRIDAY	WEEKEND

Week _____ *Year* _____

MONDAY	TUESDAY	WEDNESDAY

Quote of the Week: *Do something this week that your future self will thank you for.*

THURSDAY	FRIDAY	WEEKEND

Week _____ *Year* _____

MONDAY	TUESDAY	WEDNESDAY

Quote of the Week: *Not every closed door is locked. Push.*

THURSDAY	FRIDAY	WEEKEND

Week _____ *Year* _____

MONDAY	TUESDAY	WEDNESDAY

Quote of the Week: *Straight roads never made skillful drivers.*

THURSDAY	FRIDAY	WEEKEND

Week _____ *Year* _____

MONDAY	TUESDAY	WEDNESDAY

Quote of the Week: *You don't have to believe in miracles. Just believe in yourself.*

THURSDAY	FRIDAY	WEEKEND

Week _____ *Year* _____

MONDAY	TUESDAY	WEDNESDAY

Quote of the Week: *The secret to your future is hidden in your daily routine.*

THURSDAY	FRIDAY	WEEKEND

Week _____ *Year* _____

MONDAY	TUESDAY	WEDNESDAY

Quote of the Week: *It's hard to beat a person who never gives up.*

THURSDAY	FRIDAY	WEEKEND

Week _____ *Year* _____

MONDAY	TUESDAY	WEDNESDAY

Quote of the Week: *Don't confuse being busy with being productive.*

THURSDAY	FRIDAY	WEEKEND

Week _____ *Year* _____

MONDAY	TUESDAY	WEDNESDAY

Making mistakes is better than faking perfection.

THURSDAY	FRIDAY	WEEKEND

Week _____ *Year* _____

MONDAY	TUESDAY	WEDNESDAY

THURSDAY	FRIDAY	WEEKEND

Week _____ *Year* _____

MONDAY	TUESDAY	WEDNESDAY

Quote of the Week: *There are no shortcuts to any place worth going.*

THURSDAY	FRIDAY	WEEKEND

Week _____ *Year* _____

MONDAY	TUESDAY	WEDNESDAY

Quote of the Week: *Grateful for where I'm at, excited about where I'm going.*

THURSDAY	FRIDAY	WEEKEND

Week _____   *Year* _____

MONDAY	TUESDAY	WEDNESDAY

Quote of the Week: *Keep the promises you make to yourself.*

THURSDAY	FRIDAY	WEEKEND

Week _____ *Year* _____

MONDAY	TUESDAY	WEDNESDAY

Quote of the Week: *You are bigger than what is making you anxious.*

THURSDAY	FRIDAY	WEEKEND

Week _____ *Year* _____

MONDAY	TUESDAY	WEDNESDAY

THURSDAY	FRIDAY	WEEKEND

Week _____ *Year* _____

MONDAY	TUESDAY	WEDNESDAY

Quote of the Week: *You miss 100% of the shots you don't take.*

THURSDAY	FRIDAY	WEEKEND

Week _____ *Year* _____

MONDAY	TUESDAY	WEDNESDAY

Quote of the Week: *Old ways will not open new doors.*

THURSDAY	FRIDAY	WEEKEND

Week _____ *Year* _____

MONDAY	TUESDAY	WEDNESDAY

Quote of the Week: *Surround yourself with people who lift you up.*

THURSDAY	FRIDAY	WEEKEND

Week _____ *Year* _____

MONDAY	TUESDAY	WEDNESDAY

Quote of the Week: *When you lose your excuses, you start to find results.*

THURSDAY	FRIDAY	WEEKEND

Week _____ *Year* _____

MONDAY	TUESDAY	WEDNESDAY

Quote of the Week: *As long as you are learning, you are not failing.*

THURSDAY	FRIDAY	WEEKEND

Week _____ *Year* _____

MONDAY	TUESDAY	WEDNESDAY

Quote of the Week: *Don't look back. You're not going that way.*

THURSDAY	FRIDAY	WEEKEND

Week _____ *Year* _____

MONDAY	TUESDAY	WEDNESDAY

Your habits decide your future – act accordingly.

THURSDAY	FRIDAY	WEEKEND

Week _____ *Year* _____

MONDAY	TUESDAY	WEDNESDAY

THURSDAY	FRIDAY	WEEKEND

Week _____ *Year* _____

MONDAY	TUESDAY	WEDNESDAY

THURSDAY	FRIDAY	WEEKEND

Week _____ *Year* _____

MONDAY	TUESDAY	WEDNESDAY

Quote of the Week: *Most of the things you're worrying about won't happen.*

THURSDAY	FRIDAY	WEEKEND

Week _____ *Year* _____

MONDAY	TUESDAY	WEDNESDAY

Quote of the Week: *If your dreams don't scare you, they aren't big enough.*

THURSDAY	FRIDAY	WEEKEND

Week _____ *Year* _____

MONDAY	TUESDAY	WEDNESDAY

Quote of the Week: *Greatness never comes from comfort zones.*

THURSDAY	FRIDAY	WEEKEND

Week _____ *Year* _____

MONDAY	TUESDAY	WEDNESDAY

Quote of the Week: *Let your past make you better, not bitter.*

THURSDAY	FRIDAY	WEEKEND

Week _____   *Year* _____

MONDAY	TUESDAY	WEDNESDAY

Quote of the Week: *Believe in your own magic.*

THURSDAY	FRIDAY	WEEKEND

Week _____ *Year* _____

MONDAY	TUESDAY	WEDNESDAY

Quote of the Week: *Starve your distractions. Feed your focus.*

THURSDAY	FRIDAY	WEEKEND

Week _____ *Year* _____

MONDAY	TUESDAY	WEDNESDAY

Quote of the Week: *There is no elevator to success. You have to take the stairs.*

THURSDAY	FRIDAY	WEEKEND

Week _____ *Year* _____

MONDAY	TUESDAY	WEDNESDAY

THURSDAY	FRIDAY	WEEKEND

Week _____ *Year* _____

MONDAY	TUESDAY	WEDNESDAY

Quote of the Week: *You can't please everyone and it's a losing game to try.*

THURSDAY	FRIDAY	WEEKEND

Week _____ *Year* _____

MONDAY	TUESDAY	WEDNESDAY

THURSDAY	FRIDAY	WEEKEND

Week _____ *Year* _____

MONDAY	TUESDAY	WEDNESDAY

Quote of the Week: *The best luck of all is the luck you make for yourself.*

THURSDAY	FRIDAY	WEEKEND

Week _____   *Year* _____

MONDAY	TUESDAY	WEDNESDAY

Quote of the Week: *Success is never an accident, it's a choice.*

THURSDAY	FRIDAY	WEEKEND

Week _____   *Year* _____

MONDAY	TUESDAY	WEDNESDAY

Stay close to people that inspire you.

THURSDAY	FRIDAY	WEEKEND

Week _____ *Year* _____

MONDAY	TUESDAY	WEDNESDAY

Quote of the Week: *Read more books, ask more questions, listen more closely.*

THURSDAY	FRIDAY	WEEKEND

Week _____   *Year* _____

MONDAY	TUESDAY	WEDNESDAY

Quote of the Week: *Never feel bad about doing what's best for you.*

THURSDAY	FRIDAY	WEEKEND

Week _____ *Year* _____

MONDAY	TUESDAY	WEDNESDAY

Quote of the Week: *Tough times don't last, tough people do.*

THURSDAY	FRIDAY	WEEKEND

Week _____ *Year* _____

MONDAY	TUESDAY	WEDNESDAY

Quote of the Week: *Be fearless in the pursuit of what sets your soul on fire.*

THURSDAY	FRIDAY	WEEKEND

Week _____ *Year* _____

MONDAY	TUESDAY	WEDNESDAY

Quote of the Week: *A winner is a loser who tried one more time.*

THURSDAY	FRIDAY	WEEKEND

Week _____ *Year* _____

MONDAY	TUESDAY	WEDNESDAY

Quote of the Week: *Some days you just have to create your own sunshine.*

THURSDAY	FRIDAY	WEEKEND

Week _____ *Year* _____

MONDAY	TUESDAY	WEDNESDAY

Quote of the Week: *Raise your standards and the universe will meet you there.*

THURSDAY	FRIDAY	WEEKEND

Notes

Notes

Notes

Notes

Made in the USA
Monee, IL
13 June 2021

71193277R10063